Divinely Inspired Very Anointed

Inspirational Poems for Different Occasions and Life Situations

Volume II

By Luria Tye

Divinely Inspired Very Anointed

Inspirational Poems for Different Occasions and Life Situations

Volume II

By Luria Tye

Publishing Assistance by
R.R.H. Creation
P.O. Box 800 Monee, Il. 60449
rrhcreation@aol.com

Copyright © 2015 by Luria Tye
All Right Reserved
Reproduction of content of this book in whole or in part without the expressed written consent by the author is not permitted and is unlawful.

ISBN 978-0-9910463-1-7

Dedication

This book is first and foremost dedicated to my first love, which is my Lord and Savior Jesus Christ. It is He who has been my biggest inspiration. Because of His love, concern and compassion for me, I am able to lavish love, concern and compassion on others.

It is through His word that I find the words to enlighten and encourage you, because of the joy He has placed inside of me I am able to write these poems with a sometimes grieved, but joyful spirit. I hope that makes sense to you. My spirit is grieved sometimes because of the struggles of life one must go through and how sometimes they are overtaken by it, but at the same time my spirit is joyful in knowing I am enlightening someone by means of these poems and encouraging them on how to overcome and attain victory through Christ Jesus.

I also get joy in knowing that these poems are shared by you to help encourage or inspire your loved ones and or friends, be it by means of a Happy Birthday poem or an I Appreciate You one.

At this moment I would like to dedicate this book to my sons, Joshua, Cornilis and Amos Tye, to my mother Luria Jackson who is a great woman of strength, to my Grandmother Susie Berry who has raised me to be the woman that I am today, to my grandchildren Jahreese, LaMia, Jashaun and Calia Tye, to my sister Dorothy Wright who continuously assist me in making my books a success, to my brother Vincent Martin and to my other siblings as well. I also would like to dedicate this book to my niece Diane Murphy.

Lastly, but most definitely just as importantly, I would like to dedicate this book to every recipient that will come in contact with these poems, whether you are a recipient through the reading or hearing of these poems. My prayer is that you would be enlightened, light would overshadow darkness in your life, your heart be filled with joy and that your spirit will find liberty.

Prelude

My prayer is that these poems are a blessing to the readers and the hearers. I pray that the Anointing of God be so strongly upon these poems each and every time they are read or heard. I pray that through the reading or hearing of these poems that you would feel the love, sincerity, concern and importance of your very existence, if for no other reason, just because you are a created being, created by God!

However these poems may reach you, whether out of an act of kindness from a stranger, a friend, church or family member, I pray that you are touched by the Spirit of God. As you read or hear these poems, allow God's Spirit to mend your broken heart, lighten your burden, open your eyes, and make your faith even stronger. My prayer also is that you would see your self-worth, or see yourself at your worst, to become a better person. I pray that your will and desire will no longer be yours, but become God's will and desire as you search for the truth and a newness of life. May God's favor forever rest upon you!

Luria Tye

Divinely Inspired Very Anointed
Inspirational Poems for Different Occasions and Life Situations
Volume II

Table of Content

Jesus Is Not A Weekend Lover 1
My Treasure of Love (In Memory Of My Grandma) 3
I No Longer Fear 5
Teach Me, Oh Lord- A Parent Prayer 6
What My Church Means to Me 7
Time 9
The Gift Of A Precious Mother 10
Demons 11
Four Verses Forty- HAPPY 40TH BIRTHDAY 13
The Game Of Deceit 15
My Oldest Child 17
Where Is Your Hope 19
For life 21
Who Will Cry For Me 22
The Hidden Secret Of What This Word Would Do ... 24
A Virtuous Woman 26
A Great Inspiration 28
Summoned By God- Directed By The Holy Ghost ... 29
Never Give Up All Of You- In Your Pursuit Of Love .. 31
Be Encourage 33
The Truth Revealed 35
A Promise To My Wife 37
Heaven's Earthly Angel- HAPPY 2ND BIRTHDAY 38
Family And Friends Day 39

Table of Contents Continued

What's In A Marriage	40
Merry Christmas	42
Look Toward Heaven And See What I See	43
Terrible Two- HAPPY 2ND BIRTHDAY	45
Let Me Speak Life To You	46
You're Not Alone	48
Our Families	49
What Pride Means To Me- Work Performance	51
What It Seems Like Is Not What It Really Is	52
Wedding Day	54
Your Condition Is Not Your Conclusion	55
A Special Niece	57
Being A Minister Of Music	58
Memories- When I Met My Husband	59
When Pastors Gone Wrong	60
Favor Keep Falling In My Favor	62
Happy Dad's Day	63
Keeping It Real	64
Be Blessed	66
Gossiper	67
How Do I Let Go	69
I Just Wanted To Say Thank You	70
When Death Has Called My Name	72
No Limit	73
Extraordinary Love	74
Jealousy	75
My Prayer	76

Divinely Inspired Very Anointed

Inspirational Poems for Different Occasions and Life Situations

Volume II

By Luria Tye

Jesus Is Not A Weekend Lover

So many people are so busy in life; beginning at the start of their day, that only when it's time to settle down, they realize, I forgot to pray.

They begin to reason with the Lord as they make preparation to crawl into bed. One of their favorite sayings is: Lord, please don't charge this to my heart, but charge it to my head.

They begin to explain to Him all the things they had to do. Jesus is already shaking His head, saying to Himself even before they can get started, yeah, yeah, yeah I heard that before. Now tell me something new.

They say, you know all things Lord. You know I had to start my day with so much on my list to do. Unfortunately one of those things on my list wasn't to seek or pray to you.

As they went down their list, they said, don't worry Lord on Saturdays and Sundays you know I got you cover. Jesus replied in their spirit and said; I am not a weekend lover.

They begin to reply back to Jesus and say, but Lord! Sometimes there is not enough time to schedule prayer into my busy day, most of the time I am up and about, trying to make a way.

Jesus said, you never take the time throughout the course of the day: to spend some quality time with me, to hear what I might have to say. Then He said, oh yes! I can remember a time when you called on me, and you wanted me to come

right away.
I wanted to assist you in your time of trouble, but Mary also needed me that day. You see, Mary takes the time to read the word and in and out of season she does pray. So, when the both of you were calling on me, I had to make haste her way.

Jesus said I can remember another time when you were down to your last dime and you didn't know what to do. You waited on the weekend to call on me, but by then Johnny needed me too.

Johnny is a man who loves the Lord and in God's word he does cuddle. He finds peace, rest, joy, and strength in the Lord's word, he doesn't search for it in any other.

Now, I don't want this poem to be confusing, Jesus can bless both you and me at the same time. The moral of this poem is, to seek Jesus and you shall find.

However, Jesus is not going to allow you to keep keeping Him under cover, for He is not a forbidden love, as if He were a weekend lover.

My Treasure Of Love
(In Memory Of My Grandma)

Grandma, there is so much that has taken place in my life. Some of life situations were not too pleasant, but there were some that I wish you were here to see. I want you to know the day that Jesus called you home you also took a part of me.

You took me in as your baby and you treated me like gold. You held me and cuddled me and made me a part of your very soul.

You never made me feel as if you regretted what you had done, neither did you ever mention about it twice. Even though there were so many times I knew you had to sacrifice.

Grandma, you have always been my guardian angel from heaven up above. You have always been to me, my treasure of love.

When you departed this world I felt so all alone. But one of the things you taught me was how to be strong.

You also taught me how to be content without settling for less and how to hold out until good got better and better became best.

Grandma, you couldn't afford to give me a lot of material things and that was alright with me. Because what you have given me money can't buy. And that was your heart, your soul, your wisdom, all these things to my life I am able to apply.

I know I was selfish: I didn't want you to leave me, although I knew you were in pain and your spirit was tired and wanted to be free.

But still I ponder in my heart, what in the world could you and God been thinking of? I'm sure you both must have known that you were my treasure of love?

Many may come and go in my life, but no one could ever take your place. There will never be another you that could fill or occupy your space.

Now I say to you, rest on, sleep on, and continue on laying your head in Jesus' lap, because it really doesn't matter that you are now in heaven up above, because you will always be to me, my treasure of love.

I No Longer Fear

I have a new motto, a new saying this year, and that is I no longer fear.

I will not continue to allow the devil to keep me bound and I will no longer take my thoughts and bury them in the ground.

God has imparted encouraging words in me, words that will help to defeat the enemy.

Words that will up lift someone's spirit, strengthen someone's faith and words that will help to mend someone's broken heart.

These words must be heard! God never intended for anyone to be under the attack of Satan where he has their mind mentally or spiritually disturb.

I have a new motto, a new saying this year. I speak boldness to my spirit so I no longer fear.

I am as bold as a lion in Jesus Christ, because all things are possible with Him in my life.

I have a new motto, a new saying this year. I have taken my authority over the enemy and I have shifted it into gear.

I have decided to do what God has called me to do, and that is to speak His word unto you.

I have a new motto a new saying this year. God has empowered me with boldness so I no longer fear.

Teach Me, Oh Lord (A Parent's Prayer)

Teach me, Oh Lord, and show me the way, how to deal with my children each and every day.

Help me to understand what's on their mind. Teach me, Oh Lord, to be loving, patient and kind.

Give me an understanding of the struggles they go through. And when I don't quite understand Lord, please give me the mind to pray and ask, what would Jesus do?

Teach me, Oh Lord, as each awaking day goes by, how to discern the spirit that's in them, that makes them sad, mysterious, lonely or cry.

Teach me, Oh Lord, the things I need to know, that would help my children succeed in life, to be fruitful and grow.

Teach me, Oh Lord, how to release the favor of God to rest upon them each day. That God's angels would encamp round about them, when Satan desires to get in their way.

Teach me, Oh Lord, to deal with their individual needs. For I realize although they come from the same package, they're like individual seeds.

Each has their own personality that reflects who they are. So teach me, Oh Lord, to use wisdom, knowledge and understanding, when I begin to discipline, teach, encourage or rebuke, that I may not leave a scar.

And finally, Oh Lord, when I begin to get in your way, teach me to step aside, that I may receive the teaching that I've asked and allow your spirit to be my guide.

What My Church Means To Me

What my church meant to me, was a question I was asked. At first I thought it would be very hard to be precise and direct.

Then I sat and thought for a while about the people that resides, because we are the church, not the building that Jesus lives inside.

So I let my mind reminisce down through the years and I thought about so many people who comforted me through my trials, tribulations, persecutions and fears.

Some are still here today and others are gone away, but the memory of them all is forever in my heart to stay.

The memories are not only of sorrows, but also of laughter that we shared. Now that I really think about it, there were so many people that really cared.

I don't only mean to speak in the past, for now is a brand new day. There have been so many that have passed my path, but only some were meant to stay.

Now at this moment I would like to take the time to recognize my pastor and his wife. These are two of the most instrumental people, who have instructed, encourage, and given me sound advice.

I know I can turn to the both of them in times of trouble. Whatever the situation may be that leads to my distress, although I try within all my power not to rob them of their rest.

There is so much I could say, but this is just a poem and we the people are the body of Christ, therefore, I must also talk about the legs, feet, hands and arms.

Under the authority of God, our pastor is the great head of this body with his anointed wife by his side. However, have you ever seen a head on a body with no nose, mouth, ears or eyes?

Therefore, I must include the church as a whole and speak to those who have never been told.

I must tell everyone just how much you all mean to me and that I wish you all love, joy, good health, peace and prosperity.

So many of you have touched my life down through the years, you have inspired me with your ways of living, your dedication of consecration and how you have persevered.

You have given me encouraging words, when I was spiritually blinded and could not see. You have prayed me through so many obstacles, when Satan sent his demonic forces out to attack me.

So many of you have set the example of how a true Christian should be. So in words of short, I love and appreciate you all. A body of love is what my church means to me.

Time

Time could be a splendid thing, if respected for what it is, no matter what it consists of, one day or many years.

Time, although a four letter word that seems so small in size, plays a humongous part in our lives, and that we all must recognize.

If you would at this very moment think about everything we do, it's all on a time frame concerning me or you.

No matter how we try to speed it up or want to slow it down, time is not a punk that can be push around.

Time has value, in which no price can meet, time is constantly moving until it is complete.

Now I want you to take the time to consider this.
You can't stop the night from falling nor can you stop
the break of day, now shouldn't that be a clue? That
you are not in control of time, but time is in control of you.

Now, the reason I spoke on time is, I know some of you
have petitions that you have laid before the throne of grace.
You have been seeking, praying, trusting and believing in God,
but still it seems like you're losing the race.

Time is just a limited period, how long, I can't explain.
But if you would only continue to trust in God, He will
shelter you from the rain.

Remember, God is a problem solver, to Him it doesn't matter of what kind. He will bless you in due season and you will reap if you faint not. So why not wait on time, one thing for sure, you cannot rush or stop the clock.

So, as you go through your waiting periods of life, I want you to keep this in mind, waiting on time is not wasted time, it's just a matter of time.

The Gift Of A Precious Mother

The gift of a precious mother, could there ever be one as precious as you? There are not enough words in my vocabulary to express the honor that you're due.

The sincere-ness of your love; the warmth of your heart, the smile on your face, the strength that you discharge, all of these characteristics are descriptions of you and no one can display them as well as you do.

Nothing in this world, no silver or no gold, can outweigh the gift of the title that you hold.

The gift of a precious mother, for I have really been blessed. To know I have you in my life makes my worries so much less.

You have always been there for me no matter what the tide. Even when you didn't understand, you still stood by my side.

For that, I say, thank you and I love you too. I thank the Lord for the precious gift He has given me in you.

I wouldn't trade it for fame or fortune, neither for silver or gold. You are such a priceless gift that could never ever be sold.

Demons

The cry of demons, let us alone, has caused many broken homes.

It cries attention or reject. It can fool the very elect.

Demons are real and powerful, you see, they can take control of both you and me.

They know how to hit in all the right places. They know how to fill up empty spaces.

Some of the demons are Fear, Loneliness and Pride. They know just where to live and hide.

They come in groups and work together so well. They will cause you not to know heads from tails.

The Fear Demon keeps you in doubt. It will not let you be sure of what you're all about.

It keeps you in fear of what you can do. It makes you become dependent upon others and vulnerable too.

The Lonely Demon works so hard, to make you want to stay apart, apart from friends and everyone else, that's including your loved ones, the world itself.

The Lonely Demon carries a friend, which is Self-Pity that works within.

It makes you feel like you are not worth a dime. It makes you feel like, why me all the time?

Now we have a demon called Pride, an enemy to self. It makes you think you are better than everyone else.

No! They cannot do it as well as I can, because I am the key person. I make the plan.

Pride has a friend and his name is Ego and he shows up with pride everywhere he goes.

Ego says I am better than he or she and no one can do anything to outdo me.

So, beware my friends of these demons within and have no doubt they can be cast out.

Just remember what I say unto you. Demons come in groups not just one or two.

Four Verses Forty

Bring out the ice-cream, cake, cookies, balloons and clowns!
Oh, I'm sorry, that was when your fourth birthday had rolled around.

Now you're celebrating another birthday that is at hand.
And you're no longer a child, but a forty-year-old man.

My-oh-my what a big difference a zero makes in a number.
From four to forty should really make you sit and wonder.

As your mind flashes back over the scenes of your life,
how many things have you done that you wouldn't mind redoing twice?

How many places have you gone that you would like to revisit again? And how many friends have you had who has really stuck by you to the end?

How many lessons in life was a lesson well learned?
And how much good have you invested in someone else's life, without expecting something in return?

I know it's a big transition from playing with marbles: toy trucks, toy cars and paper planes, to taking on life challenges, enjoying the sunshine and crying in the rain.

However, whatever condition life has found you in, in this fortieth year, if you have not already, you must now take off your little boy mask and put on your forty-year-old man gear.

Which are Salvation, Wisdom and Knowledge,
Understanding, Patience, Stability and Endurance.
By wearing these as your clothing of life, you will conquer many things, that's God's assurance.

Therefore, whatever has happened in your life between the age of four and forty, just know it's up to you whether what's to come would be better than what has been. But, when you decide to take on these characteristics you will be able to stand tall against the most influential and prominent of all men.

Remember the words of Paul in 1st Corinthians 13:11
When I was a child, I spake as a child, I understood as a child, I thought as a child: but when I became a man, I put away childish things.

The Game Of Deceit

Deceit is a serious and dangerous game. It has caused many broken homes and diminishes the most prestige and common people to shame.

It is a game of destruction, lies, disloyalty and neglect. Deceit is a game of chance that I haven't seen anyone conquer yet.

Some people thought they knew the game so well, ask them today, they would have a story to tell.

Some would say I studied the game both night and day. I took notes to make sure things would go my way.

I have watched others as they did play. Never did I think deceit would play me one day.

Deceit is a master of its own game. It has been around since Adam, Eve, Able and Cain.

Deceit has made many believe what's done in the dark will never come to the light. In short, what deceit will do is take away your sight.

Deceit has its own distorted version of what you can get away with in life, just ask any doctor, lawyer, police officer, friend, neighbor, husband or wife.

Most would tell you what they lost was much greater than what they have gained. Deceit has caused them much dishonor, sorrow, grief, heartache and pain.

Deceit has caused them to lose respect from the ones most dearly to them and from others. Some have even found themselves in disbelief, while lying in strange gutters.

Deceit will strip you of all of your pride, leaving you naked with nowhere to hide.

Deceit will change your whole course of life, so before you play the game please think twice.

If I play the game and should happen to lose, are the repercussions and consequences what I really choose?

My Oldest Child

Let me tell you a little bit about my oldest child. I would like to start off by saying; I love this child very much. This child of mine is very special and has a warm and gentle touch.

There's nothing I could ever ask, that I don't believe this child wouldn't try to do. This child of mine has a heart of gold and this child's love for me is pure and genuine too.

My oldest child sometimes amazes me, because there are times when my child seems wise beyond one's years. I tell you, if you got to know this child, you would see that there's more to this child than what appears.

My oldest child I must say is very pleasing to the eye. To look into my child's face, is like looking at the beauty of the stars in the sky.

My oldest child keeps me smiling all of the time. When this child enters into the room, it's like a radiance of sunshine.

My oldest child will always be a reminder to me, of how I am blessed and how God decided to by-pass the good and the better and give me the best.

There might be one who is thinking to themselves, I am just saying and doing what mothers do. But please continue to listen to this poem, believe me when I tell you I am not through.

I know it seems like I am making this child out to be a human without a fault. Clearly you must understand, that is not the thought.

My oldest child, like you and I, have flaws as well: for instance, when this child of mine gets one little ache, oh! There's a story to tell.

A paper cut on the finger, a petty stump of the toe, has stopped this child of mine from performing at its best. Because this child is in so much agony, the pain has now robbed this child out of all of its rest.

Now, I know I said my oldest child is very special and there's nothing for me this child wouldn't do. But sometimes I swear to you, this child acts the age of one or two.

Breaks of a fingernail, from just the simplest pain, in this child of mine no strength can be gained.

No dishes can be washed; no floors can be mopped, no garbage taken out. I know some of you know what I'm talking about.

Ok, I know I have been exaggerating but, I think it should be made known, that my oldest child is way passed grown.

Although my oldest child is not my child by blood, as days grew into weeks, so did my love.

For those of you who have been listening patiently and allowing me to vent for a while, can you believe my husband is my oldest child?

Where Is Your Hope

Where is your hope, in whom does it lie? Is your hope based on what you see with the eye?

Where is your hope, tell me what do you confess? Is your hope built on the word and nothing less?

When nights are lonely and clouds are dark; do you still have enough hope to believe in your heart that, Jesus is the great I Am?

Whatever you need Him to be, rather its food or shelter, joy or peace or a lamp beneath your feet.

When your friends and loved ones turn and walk away, do you still have hope to face yet another day?

When the doctor says there is nothing I can do, do you use your faith to carry you through?

Now hope and faith go hand in hand. In order to have hope you must have faith to know that God can.

God can be your company keeper late in the midnight hour. God can be the source of your strength connected to the Holy Ghost Power.

Where is your hope, in whom does it lie in time of desperate needs? Do you turn and depend on man, or fall down on your knees?

When your mate has left and the bills are due and your children are gone astray, do you use your hope and faith in God to lead and guide the way?

When you have prayed all night long and everything is still going wrong, Psalm thirty-seven and seven says, "Rest in the Lord, and Wait." That is the time you must be patient and use your shield of faith.

For God said I am the Lord thy God, and in Him He wants you to trust. But if you throw away your faith, and let go of your hope, downhill is surely a must.

For Life

As we come together this day, to be united as husband and wife, and as we take our vows of love before the minister, others and Christ,

I want you to know that my heart is overwhelmed with the joy of knowing I'll soon be your wife. And there's no greater thought I would rather entertain than the one of you and I together, forever, for life.

I thank God for choosing me, to be the one He chose for you, and my daily prayer will always be that our love would forever be new.

For I realize the vows we make are not what makes us one, nor our marriage complete. But it's the love, respect, communication, joy and pain that we will share with one another that will keep our marriage strong and unique.

Can you imagine the sun rising on a summer day and the stars sparkling at night? Then you can imagine the beauty of it all, of the thought of being your wife.

And just as these rings we will present to each other, which is of a circle that has no end. That is the way my love is for you, my husband to be, my lover, my best friend.

Yes, I've said it once and now the time has come for me to repeat it twice, I cannot imagine it being any other way, than you and I together, forever, for life.

Who Will Cry For Me?

Imagine a little child who's spirit should be totally free, would have to ask the question, who will cry for me?

Their pain is more than they can explain: their joy has been taken away; the darkness that has been placed over their life has overthrown their will to play.

I know a child's parents are supposed to be the first protector of their own. But, what if it's the child's parents who have left them to face life all alone?

Be it out of willingness or something out of the parent's control, should that child be pushed aside, as if they had no mind, body or soul?

Should that child be left in this world with no hope of their spirit ever being free? And the only words they can utter out of their mouth are, who will cry for me?

Should they wonder who will embrace them in their arms and provide them love and care, who will wipe away their tears, and all their pains are willing to share?

Imagine a little child whose spirit should be totally free; has lost all will to live and their dreams are tossed and driven like the waves in the sea.

The bible says, it is God's will that a child be born. A child represents life and their life should be worry free. Their mind should never have to wonder, who will cry for me?

Would you be the one who will mend a broken heart?
That at an early age that child could proclaim, there is a God?

Or, will you walk away and pretend these things you do not see; and that child's daily thought continues, who will cry for me?

Will you be the one who says, enough! Another soul Satan will not steal. I will cry for you. Oh yes! I will.

The Hidden Secrets Of What This Word Will Do (Unforgiveness)

There's no doubt in my mind there is a time in your life where someone has done you wrong. But what didn't kill you in the process should have made you strong.

I believe I know what happened to you in between the two. Satan whispered in your ear and spoke a word to you.

He took this word and he began beautifying it up, but what he didn't tell you was that this word meant self-destruct.

He told you to take this word and hide it in your heart and to leave it there to death due you part.

He told you that this word rightfully belonged to you, but what he didn't tell you, was the hidden secrets of what this word will do.

This word is very powerful and it will control your every action at its command. It will destroy all what's good in you and on your face you're destined to land.

This word will cause you to be sick and the doctors wouldn't even be able to find a reason why. It will put you in a state of confusion, where you don't know rather to laugh or cry.

This word will leave you bitter, lonely and depressed. It will take away all of your joy and replace it with distress.

This word will not allow you to be a conqueror of what God has in store for you. Why? Because there are so many hidden secrets of what this word will do.

This word has been known to torture the one in whom it resides. It has been known to eat you up and bury you alive.

Its master will allow this word to use you to the capacity. Then he will laugh in your face and say: if only you would have asked of me.

What are the hidden secrets of what this word will do? Even though I wouldn't have been honest and told you what was true.

You see, I am a liar and the truth I can't release. You should have gone to Jesus and sought Him for your peace.

Now that you know that Satan is a liar and his words can never be true, have you figured out by now what has been happening to you?

The word is unforgiveness. You have used it as a guide. You have given it permission to stick right by your side.

You must now release the power of unforgiveness by renouncing it in your heart. You must speak God's word of love and tell unforgiveness, this day you will depart.

For love always covers a multitude of faults. You must now look unto Jesus for healing and keep Him in your thoughts.

You must tell Satan he will no longer have dominion and power over you. Why? Because, now you know the hidden secret of what unforgiveness will do.

A Virtuous Woman

Proverbs thirty-one and ten asks who can find a virtuous woman. That lets me know there are very few. But when I think of a virtuous woman, my mind reflects on you.

A virtuous woman is known by her characteristics of love, faith, strength, wisdom, honesty and compassion. You have been proven to wear all of these as your clothing and you display them as if they were a daily fashion.

A virtuous woman has God on her mind in everything she attempts to do. When you are blessed enough to have her as a wife, mother or friend, you have something worth holding on to.

Virtuous woman, I have watched your way of living down through the years. I am a witness of your walk with Christ. You are that virtuous woman in whom her husband is proud to call his wife.

He feels your love and strength and he feels safety in your arm. He knows he can trust in you and you will never do him any harm.

A virtuous woman rises early in the morning while everyone else is asleep, Kneeling down on her bending knees, asking the Lord her family to keep.

Your children call you blessed, a woman that fears God. You have taught them the importance of prayer and how His word will never, ever dissolve.

You have shown yourself friendly to those who were in need of a friend. You have never failed to stick by their side day out or day in.

Your love and giving just don't stop there with your family and your friends. God has giving you an amazing love that seems like it has no end.

You are always ready to stretch out your hands to the poor and give what is needed to the needy. You don't wait to see who is going to do what, but your works are done speedily.

You are that virtuous woman that no one has to think of words to build you up. For the fruit of your hands speaks for itself and the life you live that is uncorrupt.

A Great Inspiration

You are a great inspiration to all, to both the young and the old.

When God shaped you in your mother's womb He put inspiration in your mode.

He knew one day you would see things His way and cross over to His side. Now here you are inspiring others to allow God to be their guide.

Ever since you have been in church, you have had a willing mind. Even the unfamiliar challenges you never did mind trying.

Not only do you work with your own auxiliary, but you also volunteer your services to the entire ministry, you have no respect of person, there is not a one too great or small.

God has giving you a willing Spirit to love and serve us all.

You not only inspire us with your work of many deeds.
You also give encouraging words to those who are in need.

You let us know that Christ is the answer for every situation and there is no failure in Him at all, we must learn to be patient.

Now it's my turn to encourage you to continue to inspire and encourage others no matter where you may meet, whether it's in your home, on your job, in your church or on the street.

Someone is in need of inspiration to help them through their day. You are one of the ones God has chosen to help inspire them along the way.

Summoned By God; Directed By The Holy Ghost

We have been summoned by God to fight in this war and defeat the enemy at hand. God has a road map for us to follow and He's sketched out a perfect plan.

We know the enemy comes but to kill, steal, and destroy, and to take that which is good away. Just like being in the natural army, we have to prepare ourselves each day.

God hasn't only summoned us, but He has left us a leader in charge. He has told us to be directed by the Holy Ghost and obey it with all of our heart.

The Holy Ghost will not fail; in fact, it will direct us in what to do. It will tell us what our weapons are and how to defeat the enemy too.

First of all: the weapons of our warfare are not carnal, but they are mighty through God. There is no way we can fight in the flesh nor can we fight unguarded.

Now there's a uniform we must wear and we must wear it to a tee. When Jesus said put on the whole armor of God, He was talking to you and me.

This armor will help us to stand against all strategies and the deceits of the devil. It will protect us from head to toe as we fight our worst scenario.

We must hold our ground and tighten up our belt, with God's word of truth. We must have on the breastplate of righteousness so God can see us through.

We must stand firmly with our feet shod with the good news of the gospel of peace, but above all, we must take the shield of faith and place the devil under our feet.

We must have on the helmet of salvation, which is the word of God. We must be ready to use it at all times to fight the enemy at lodge.

Finally, my brethren we must pray in the spirit with supplication for ourselves and all mankind that we may attain victory over the devil, which comes to destroy the body, soul and mind.

Never Give Up All Of You In Your Pursuit Of Love

We as people will have many choices in life. In our decision making we must be wise in how we love and what we choose to do. One thing I want to make plain and simple, never to anyone give up all of you.

God has designed us as humans to desire another human's love. However, He never designed, commanded or instructed us to give up our total being, not to anyone, except Him up above.

Sometimes in our pursuit of love, we love just a little too hard, and all the unseemly, ungodly ways that shows up on a person in the light, we choose to keep hidden in the dark.

Yes! We should love and honor our parents, God's word promise that it will lengthen our days upon the earth. And yes! We should love, adore and stand by our children's side, because it's to them we have given birth.

Yes! It is a pleasure and an honor to have friends that we can love, be concerned about and help out as well, but not to the point where we indulge in their lifestyle that will send our souls to hell.

Last, but most definitely not least, Yes! We should love, cherish, honor, confide in and support our spouse, because we are no longer two, but one.

But we should never make anyone our God, as if they are the reason we live, move and have our being, because if Jesus chooses to speak one word, on this earth again we will never be seen.

So never give up all of you in your pursuit of love. For if you give up all of you, what's left for your heavenly father up above?

Be Encouraged

This poem is to encourage a person such as you. Who is always encouraging others when needing encouraging too.

Never saying I am having a bad day and this is really not the time, but always willing to listen and hear what's on others minds.

Then you give a word that comes straight from your heart, but the best thing about it is it's the Word of God.

Saying thus sayeth the Lord, what He would have you to say, not sugar coating it in any type of way.

But saying it out of love, kindness and concern and explaining it in a way that even a child could learn.

This poem is to encourage a person such as you who is willing to go the extra mile, although sometimes inconvenient to do.

Sometimes sick and tired, sometime worn and frail, but always ready to do your part in helping and wishing others well.

So I want to say to you, be encouraged in all you do and know that God is pleased when you help the least of these.

These are His people, both the young and the old, in Christ or out for they are still a precious soul.

Be encouraged for your works are not in vain. There is a reward stored up for you in the heavenly realm to be release in Jesus' name.

All of your needs and your desires too, believe and trust in God to give them to you.

He knows your faith and He has seen your deeds. He is ever ready to supply your needs.

So be encouraged, God has designated a special time for your special blessing to come. But until then continue to praise our Lord and Savior, which is Christ, the Holy One.

The Truth Revealed

There is a game show called: "To Tell the Truth" and it's based on three contestants. One will tell the truth about who they really are and the other two will have false confessions.

On the panel there are four judges and they will ask a series of questions. The contestants will be judged on the promptness of their answers and their facial expressions.

Now let's pretend you are a contestant along with the other two. They have taken the time to study for the show, but to live the life they certainly didn't do.

There are two more things before we go on that I must let you know and that is the topic and the questions for today's show.

The topic is: Will The Real Woman of God Please Stand Up? Don't be alarmed or be afraid unless you are living ruthless, unseemly and very corrupt.

Now don't get me wrong, I know Satan is a great imitator of many things that Jesus do. But one more thing I feel I must let you know, and that is, these are God's angels judging you.

Now the first two questions you'll be asked are your names and for a confession of your faith. Do you have an idea of how you would answer or would there surely be a great debate?

Would you be able to say, I'm a Christian? A child of God I profess to be. Could you speak out boldly and say with all assurance, I know Jesus rose from the dead, because He rose in me?

Would there be such a conviction and seriousness on your face that the judges would know it has to be you? But just for the sake of going on with the show, they continue and say to the others, now tell me, what do you do?

The next questions that will be asked are, have you been a witness in your home, amongst your family and your friends? Is this where you have no answer and your seriousness comes to an end?

On the other hand, could you say, I have loved my husband, stood by his side and done all that you've commanded? I have witnessed to my family and my friends, and on your word only did I stand.

I have trained my children in the way they should go, under the word of God. I have taught them how to love, fast and pray, and to seek you with all their heart.

Would there be a need for more questions to be asked or would the judges say "no further we need to go" for God has revealed the real woman of God and she has already stood up on the show.

A Promise To My Wife

It is a gift, an honor and a pleasure to be joined together with you for life, and as we take this journey together, I would like to make a promise to you, my wife.

I promise to love, respect, cherish and honor you in every possible way. I promise to make our home a home of peace and a safe haven, both during the night and day.

I promise to take our vow of marriage so sacredly that it would keep you so amazed. I promise to continuously give you all of me, today, tomorrow, forever, always.

The bible says, "He who finds a wife, finds a good thing" now that I have found you, I know exactly what that means. You are a woman full of compassion, grace and so much love. If I had to describe you, it would be with the words "heaven sent from above".

You are a woman to be adorned in every aspect of the meaning of this word. There were times when you were listening, when you really should have been heard.

So, I promise never to take for granted neither you nor the love you have for me. If I could I would take all your burdens, your worries, your tears, bottle them up and throw them into the bottom of the sea.

To sum it all up and just to be precise, you are the woman I plan on growing old with for the rest of my life.

It wouldn't mean a thing if I lived to be a hundred and two and I could not share the memories of living them with you.

Heaven's Earthly Angel (HAPPY 2ND BIRTHDAY)

I heard that the angels in heaven have all gathered around to rejoice about something exciting and new. And that is, the most precious and prettiest little angel on earth has just made her arrival into the sparkling age of two.

I'm sure the angels have marked this day with their biggest star and they are flapping their wings all around. Grandma has sealed this day with her love and a kiss, and I too have been spreading the news all over town.

I realize you must be very busy, Grandma doesn't know all the things you might have planned. However, Grandma was wondering is there any way possible I could lend you a helping hand?

I promise to do as I'm told, whatever you would have me to do. After all, this is your birthday, you are the one who has entered into the amazing world of two.

Grandma would be honored if you would allow me to bake you a cake with all the ingredients of love. Like joy and laughter, funny faces and smiles, and a lot of kisses and hugs.

But just in case you don't need my help and you have already made plans with your earthly angel friends, that's quite alright Grandma understands, because with Grandma you never have to pretend.

Family and Friend's Day

This is our homecoming family and friend's day; a day of celebration. We have taken the time to set this day apart for this very special occasion.

We know family and friends are very important and we all need them in our lives. So, today we have come together as one to connect the family ties.

When I speak of family ties this does not exclude our friends. We love you all just as well and felt joy when you walked in.

Now, family and friends we have invited you here to join us in all we do. However, one important thing we must all remember, we have invited Jesus here too.

Everything we do, we must do decently and in order, so when our elder brother reports to our father, He could still be proud to claim us as His sons and daughters.

Let's get ready as we continue on, to sing and to shout. Let's get ready to let the sinner man know what this joy is all about.

Let's take our voices and mingle them together as we send up perfect praise. Let's have a good time in the Holy Ghost and keep the devil in a great daze.

Let's encourage each other in words and deeds as we go along the way. So our heavenly father will be pleased when He announces, He has recorded this family and friend's day.

What's In A Marriage

What's in a marriage? Do you have a Clue? Some people think it's just something I'll do.

What's in a marriage, tell me how you thought it out? Do really know what marriage is all about?

Do you know the part that you would have to play, being a married person, not once but every day?

Some say I'll marry just out of fun and games, others say I'll marry and I'll marry in Jesus' name.

For either one of these that you choose, let me give you a bit of heavenly news.

Marriage is a commitment that was instituted by God. When you said I do, you took on an important part.

The part you took on wasn't only to benefit you. It was to bless God, your mate and others too.

You may say, what do you mean? However, the role you play could be a great thing.

It could also be negative too. One thing for sure it's all up to you.

Do you love your spouse as you love yourself? Do you stick by them in sickness and in health?

Do you cherish and keep them in your heart or is the thought of them gone just as soon as you part?

Whatever happened to for richer or for poorer, have that vow been thrown out the door?

Had you forgotten your promise to forsake all others? Sometimes this means mother, father, sister or brother.

You also said to death do us part, some are still married but divorced in their hearts.

What's in a marriage? Do you have a clue? Did you seek the Lord for what you should do?

He said, all you do, do unto the glory of God and it shall be blessed right from the start.

God will show you just how to be. You could even ask yourself, would I want to marry me?

Treat your spouse as your earthly best friend. Love and cherish them day out and day in.

Speak words to each other that would only edify and watch the flourish of your love as it begins to multiply.

Treat your mate with dignity and respect and you will have a marriage that you will never ever regret.

Attend and cater to each other's needs, you'll soon find out how prosperous the seed.

Put something into your marriage that you may get something out, God would be blessed and others too, no doubt.

People will see the blessing upon thee and know that God is at hand. Some may even take the time to fast and pray before making such a big plan.

Therefore it's all up to thee how your marriage could be, cold or forever be new. Just pray and meditate on these things, what a married person should do.

Merry Christmas

M- Stands for the **Mercy** that God shows towards us.

E - Stands for His **Everlasting** love and His trust.

R - Stands for **Render** your life to Jesus and lay all your cares at His feet.

R - The other R stands for **Remember** all doubt and fear you must delete.

Y - Stands for **Yes** to His will and His way, and your life will Be merry, I must say.

C - Stands for **Christ** is knocking at your heart.

H - Stands for **Hope** that will never keep you and God apart.

R - Stands for **Really**, God has a plan.

I - Stands for **It's** all in your hands.

S- Stands for **Surely**, God does care.

T- Stands for **Take Time** to talk to Him in prayer.

M- Stands for **M**ake every day, a day fresh and new.

A - Stands for **A**lways know that God is near you.

S - The last S Stands for the **SAVIOR** is born and I pray that in Him you will trust and lean on.

Look Toward Heaven And See What I See

I know everything within you has told you life has been unfair. But remember the words of Jesus when He said, He wouldn't put more on you than you are able to bare.

Although you know there are many around that love you somehow that just doesn't ease the pain. Just remember there is peace and comfort when you call on Jesus' name.

If I had the power I would dry up all your tears.
I would give you back everything the devil has stolen from you, starting from this day and down through the years.

I would take away all of your sadness and replace it with joy. I would tell all of your worries to disappear and not to return anymore.

But since I don't have the power, for it wasn't given unto me, I want you to look towards heaven and see what I see.

I see Jesus with His arms open wide, ready to comfort and strengthen you, ready to ease your pain inside.

I hear His voice saying, my child, I love you and I will always be there. Give your heart completely to me, although it has been broken, there's nothing I can't repair.

I see Jesus wiping away all of your tears, speaking life into your spirit with full of blesseth years.

I hear Jesus saying, "I want you to reach beyond your struggles and everything negative that you see, and use your hope and faith to grab a hold to me".

I see Jesus catering to your every need and pouring you out an abundance of blessings that you won't have room to receive.

I can also hear Jesus saying, "My child, think not this is strange what you are going through. You are a living testimony and once again, I have need of you".

But just in case you need some love that is not supernatural from above.

You can always count on me, for my love is genuine and unconditionally.

Terrible Two (HAPPY 2ND BIRTHDAY)

It's that special time of year again, now you have turned two. What in the world on God's green earth, are you going to do?

I know the decision must be very hard. You haven't quite made up your little mind, but could you spare grandma just a few moments of your precious and valuable time?

They say you are at that age, what they call the terrible two, and your favorite word will be no!

It doesn't matter what anyone says to you, Grandma wants you to know, although I've found that saying to be true.

Grandma loves you with all her heart and wishes only the best for you.

Let Me Speak To You

Perhaps you have been living your life misguided, lonely, sad and depressed. I come to let you know that the devil is about to be undressed.

Words have been spoken into your spirit that has caused you so much pain. And it seems like more often than not, you can't enjoy the sunshine for the pouring of the rain.

I know the devil has told you that no one really cares and he is the only one who all your burden shares.

The devil is a liar and his words will never be true, so if you just allow me, let me speak life to you.

Jesus came that you might have life and life more abundantly. He's the one that lived and died to set your spirit free.

Perhaps someone has wronged you in such an ungodly way and in your spirit it haunts you both during the night and day.

You can remember things that has happen when you were just a little child. Please believe me when I tell you, some childhood memories don't only last for just a little while.

There are growing up stages in our lives that take us from childhood into an adult stage that we must go through. Unfortunately, as we get larger and grow older, some of our childhood problems do too.

You see, Satan's job is to deceive and his duties are to kill, steal and destroy. In him you will never find peace, your life will always be in an uproar.

I don't mean to be a pest, but I know God's word is true. So if you just allow me, let me speak life to you.

You don't have to harbor on negative things that are of the past. Harbor on the word of God: the only true thing that will last.

Jesus said He will give you peace that passeth all understanding. Just believe in Him and on His word and you will always find safe landing.

I know you might be saying, but you don't know what I've been through. Please! Do one thing for me: speak God's word of life to you.

As you speak and believe God's word and embed it in your heart, you'll begin to see how Satan's word will find no meaning or space and how it will dislodge.

You'll soon find out that God's word is powerful and sharper than any two-edge sword and has been proven to be true. Then your words would be to another hurting soul, let me speak life to you.

You're Not Alone

I know it seems like you are forgotten, but remember you are not alone. There is always a place in my heart, a place where you belong.

I know it seems like you are forgotten, but you are not alone. I talk about you in the church, at my job and in my home.

Forgotten is the word or it may seem to be. But I never can forget all the things you have done for me.

I thank God for a friend who has been as good to me as you, although I had nothing to offer, you always saw me through.

I know it seems like you are forgotten, but you are not alone. Just remember my dear friend; God is looking from His throne.

He feels your pains and sees your tears. He has heard your cries down through the years.

He knows your weakness in every way, but still He loves you day by day.

I know it seems like you are forgotten, but you are not alone. Just look up my dear one toward the mercy throne.

Our Families

Our families are a group of people in which we had no choice. These are the ones we need the most, but sometimes there is much remorse.

Families should stick together through thick and through thin. Families should always do their best to try to make amends.

Now we have our parent's family where there is a mother, father, sister, or brother. Then we have our own family by our spouse or our lover.

In any case, it may be your parent's family, comes secondly.

Not saying that you should love them any less, but now God has given you your own family to love and give your very best.

There should be love, strength and security in your home. There should be honesty, communication and peace that roam.

People should walk in your home and say it is blessed. They should feel nothing but love not any type of mess.

If there is something wrong, they shouldn't know, because the Spirit of God should fill every room they go.

Now there is Satan which intervenes, he wants you to have none of these things.

Satan knows God instituted the family before God instituted the church. That is why Satan works so hard to bring much pain and hurt.

Satan also knows out of the home come: pastors, preachers, prophets and missionaries, doctors, lawyers, scientist and others that is extraordinary.

Satan knows a strong family makes a strong society. That is why his mission in the home is to bring much anxiety.

Sometimes we have feelings that we just keep inside. We are too ashamed to let them out, so we just let them hide.

We are too proud to let our guards down to say: you hurt me, I feel rejected or used. So we just walk around year after year feeling alone and abused.

However, none of these things has to be, we have a God who is more powerful than he.

God can save and make your family a family of love. He can give them peace that comes from above.

He can take any family and make them a family that's whole. If you just allow Him, He can mend each member's wounded soul.

What Pride Means To Me (Work Performance)

When people think of the word pride, some people think of it in terms of being arrogant, conceited and over confident. What pride means to me is performing my job to the best of my ability, giving it 100 percent.

Pride could be a good thing when shown in moderation and in the right frame of mind. There is nothing wrong in the fulfillment of pride, knowing you have honestly utilized your time.

I take pride in performing my duties wherever there's a need. I get pleasure in knowing I am one of the vessels used to help this company to succeed.

And when the day has come to an end and I know I have done my best. I take pride in knowing, now I can sit and rest.

What It Seems Like Is Not What It Really Is

I know sometimes it seems that life is nothing but a struggle and you find no rest or peace being a single mother.

Your days seem long, your nights seem short and your problems are more than a few. I'm sure you have asked this question so many times, what am I going to do?

I know it seems like you have carried so much weight on your shoulders down through the years. Your road has been rough, your going has been tough and your pillow has been filled with tears.

I know sometimes it feels like no one cares about your pain or the struggles you go through. I want you to know I love you very much and I will always be here for you.

The bible tells us that our trials and tribulations come to make us strong, It doesn't always have to be the results of something we've done wrong.

But most importantly remember this, God sees and He hears the cries of His' people.

He has seen your struggles, He has felt your pain, He has heard your prayers and He knows your name.

God knows you have a hunger and thirst for righteousness and He knows the kindness of your heart. He knows the trials and tribulations that you are going through, they are planting and watering the seeds of your new harvest for your new blessings to start.

You are more than a conqueror and you have stored up blessings that are waiting to meet up with time. All you have to do is continue to trust in the Lord and ask Him for a renewal of the mind.

What it seems like is not what it really is. Remember! Satan's job is to make things delusional at all times. So that he may keep a hold on God's people by keeping a hold on their minds.

Wedding Day

May your Wedding Day be filled with grace, love and so much joy.

May you find such happiness like never ever before.

May the grace of God be with you both throughout your whole life through.

May you never look back and regret this day, but your love forever be new.

Your Condition Is Not Your Conclusion

Jesus never promised in this journey called life that there would never be any heartaches, pains or strife.

There will be dark tunnels that you will have to travel through and there will be strong storms to weather that will be unpleasant for you.

Jesus knows because of our imperfection as being human beings we will make mistakes by allowing our flesh to dictate and get in the way. And although Jesus is a forgiving God, still there will be consequences and penalties one must pay.

However, Jesus' punishment isn't meant to put us on death row: neither is it meant to be a lifetime sentence to keep us unstable, in despair, upset or in the mist of confusion. So; when you are going through your test of testimonies, remember what has already been revealed in God's word: your condition is not your conclusion.

I see you as a warrior of God, who in God's Spirit you love to embrace. I see Jesus equipping you to be an instrument He can use to help give others strength and courage to run this race.

I know you have petitions that you have laid at Jesus' feet. I want you to know it is your faith that will move Him and not your loss of sleep.

So, take your eyes off what you see and see what you know and that is the word and the works of God, which makes the devil already a defeated foe.

Remember your adversary: the devil. It is his job to fill your heart and mind with his lies as well as keep you in delusion. But I encourage you once more to stand firm on what has already been spoken to you; by way of God's word. Your condition is not your conclusion.

A Special Niece

When this poem was written, it was written with someone like you in mind. One not often blessed with a special niece like mine.

Your beauty is not only outward, but inward as well. You have been endowed with so much grace and you exhibit it very well.

This poem is for a special niece. Oh yes! This means you. I must give you honor, because honor you are due.

You have made me very proud to say at the least, to have someone like you I can call my niece.

You have gone forward when you had an excuse to quit. You made up in your mind no man can dig your ditch.

You set yourself a goal and a purpose too. You took on life's challenges as though they were nothing new.

I want to say to you, continue to stand strong and continue to build on solid ground. Do not let anyone or anything on this earth mislead or turn you around.

I love you and I wish you well, prosperity and wealth this day.

You are a special niece that deserves everything good that comes your way.

Being A Minister Of Music

Being a Minister of Music is such a beautiful role, because music is a ministry that soothes the wounded soul.

There is peace and comfort that strengthen the heart. There is encouragement and hope that leads to a brand new start.

Being a Minister of Music, that is who you are.
It's like being a radiant of sunshine or a shining star.

It brings light to where it was once so dark. It brings healing to the most scarred heart.

It gives you courage to press ahead the strength to leave the past behind. The ministry of music has its place and it has been known to be medicine for all mankind.

So, just remember each and every day, God is using you in a miraculous way.

Music set the mode for the heart to receive the word.
It increases the faith of what has been seen, said or heard.

Being a Minster of Music is a calling and a Gift that God has given you to fulfill. So, always stay in tune with God, concerning His good and perfect will.

Memories; When I Met My Husband

When I met my husband we were both very young, but we knew in our hearts something new had begun.

We were always together it seems like never ever apart, because we always had each other on our minds and in our hearts.

Talking on the telephone that was our daily routine, always feeling goose bumps when each other's face we'd seen.

When we took our walks we walked hand and hand, feeling like we were on top of the world, feeling very grand.

Driving in the car and hearing our favorite song made the days so special and the nights not very long.

When I met my husband we knew this was something new, as the years went by our love grew and grew.

Grew from puppy love into the adult stage, that's when we knew our love was pure and heaven made.

Many years has gone by and here we are today, still saying I love you in our own special way.

When Pastors Gone Wrong

A Pastor should be a person that is appointed and anointed by God, because there's an enormous obligation to his congregation at lodge.

Not only should he be a strong pillar to his congregation and the community in which he resides. But everyone that knows him should know he is a man of morals and strong family ties.

A Pastor should be a man of great faith: he must show love, commitment, authority, strength and courage as well as communication to those God has put him in charge, especially in his home.

But if a Pastor is not extremely careful, but most of all prayerful, he could find himself labeled in the Hall of Shame, of When Pastors Gone Wrong.

Some people see their Pastors as miniature Jesus in the flesh. When a Pastor has allowed this to go on, he has signed himself up for a whole lot of mess.

Some Pastors have women in their congregation falling at their feet. Some even have the nerves to ask "Pastor, outside the church can we meet?"

Not only should a Pastor be knowledgeable, but wisdom should be a factor in every case. He should never find himself alone daily one on one, in the same one woman's face.

She may say, "But Pastor there is some things I only want you to know." Wisdom should kick in and he should say; the First Lady and I are one and respect we will show.

God will give you discerning of spirits and guide you in wisdom in what to say and do. But if for some reason you are taken by surprise God will show you how to handle that too.

Yes! You have an enormous obligation to your congregation, but more of a phenomenal one to your wife. Being a First Lady isn't always easy, there's many times she too sacrifice.

When the Pastor carries the weight of the church on his shoulder, hers is often weighted down too. When they have made plans to spend time together he has to sometimes spend it with you, you and you.

But when Pastors become big-headed and see the pulpit as their throne, that's one of the signs of when Pastors gone wrong.

Just a word of warning Pastors: stay faithful to God, love your church and honor your marriage. If you choose to go the opposite way, you will soon find Mary at your front door with a baby in a baby carriage.

God instituted the family before He did the church. He has never told you to neglect your home. So don't blame God when you see your name in The Hall of Shame labeled under: "When Pastors Gone Wrong".

Favor Keeps Falling In My Favor

A wretch undone saved by grace, by the mercy of God I am still in this race.

How He came to love me so, this is one thing I will never know.

I have made my mistakes along the way and in Satan's army I did labor. But glory be to God, He who keeps me in mind, favor keep falling in my favor.

I took my youth for granted and it showed up in my behavior. I should have been buried in my grave, but death the Lord did waiver.

Not saying that you don't reap what you sow, it was only by the favor of God that I lived to be this old.

I have asked Jesus to forgive me of my sins, to enlist me in His army and to take me in.

For every negative thing that could have happened to me that I've escaped: I know it was Jesus who was on my side. For even now there are doors that could and should have been shut tightly, my Lord and Savior have kept them open wide.

So, I will bless the Lord at all times, because He is my life saver. Even when I don't deserve it favor keep falling in my favor.

Happy Dad's Day

The phrase, "Happy Father's Day", for some men the word father is just a one word title.

Any man could be a father and it doesn't take much either. A father doesn't wear many hats as I see you do. So I would like to change the phrase and say: Happy Dad's Day to you!

I see you as a dad who has shown his children what it means to have dignity: a sense of direction and determination, a dad who has stood by his children's side through their proudest times and challenging moments without any hesitation.

Because of the love and support you have shown your children, they are not reluctant to call on you for fatherly advice. For they value your opinion and the role you have and continue to play in their life.

Yes, I implied the word father, I can't take anything from you, because you have earned and deserve that title too. But I see you as so much more than that, for that reason I say, Happy Dad's Day to you!

You are a dad with a positive attitude, one who believes in using it to allow yourself to reach the highest altitude of your expectation.

I rate you as being the number one dad, when it comes to being to your children of great inspiration.

Your durability, dependability, and distinctiveness have caused you to rise above being called more than just a father. So, again I say, Happy Dad's Day baby! A shout out to my baby, Holler!!!

Keeping It Real

Have you ever wondered about this Christian journey that we are traveling through? Have you ever questioned the Lord about some of the things that have happen to you?

Have you ever sat and cried because you didn't understand why? Have you ever felt an emotional pain so badly, you thought it was just better to die?

Have you ever been in a state of mind where you didn't know what to do and your every thought was: why was the Lord allowing this to happen to you?

Have you ever lost your temper to the point where you did or said something you knew you would soon regret? Have you ever been in love with someone you wish you had never ever met?

Have you ever reached the point that being a Christian had lost its appeal? If the truth be told, many of these things have happened to the best of us. I'm just keeping it real.

Being a Christian doesn't mean we are perfect neither does it mean we are never under the weather. Sometimes our faith is shaken, our hearts are broken and we too have days when we struggle to keep things together.

There were times in my life when I had to fake a smile. There were times when I pondered in my heart was this Christian's life worthwhile.

There was a point and time in my life when I had lost my Christian's zeal. Please don't look at me funnily or judge me. Unlike you, I'm just keeping it real.

There may be a time when you are led by the spirit to testify about your life challenges and although you may be looking all dignified and as some may say, dressed to kill, regardless of who may or who may not understand. Just say to them all, I'm just keeping it real.

Be Blessed

For someone who is as sweet as you, may all your dreams and hopes come true.

May this day and all your years be filled with peace that over take your fears.

May God's angels protect and keep you safe every second of the day. May you never forget to seek what is His will and perfect way.

May you find peace in all the right places. May you allow the Holy Spirit to fill up your empty spaces.

May you always know that deep in my heart, my prayer for you is to be blessed by God.

Gossiper

Gossiping has always been one of my favorite pass time things. I look forward to hearing the phone or when the doorbell rings.

I don't care whom it hurts or the nature of the talk, as long as I can gossip about it, that's what I'm talking about.

It could be about your mama, my mama, the milkman, the postman, the garbage man or even all about you. And ask me if I care or not, rather or not it's true.

Some people say Gossiper should have been my first, middle and last name. Well, I must admit when it comes to gossiping my name should have been placed in the Hall Of Fame.

So don't get mad at me when you tell me your personal business as well as other people's secrets too, although you may have related to me, this is between me and you.

You should have known the M.O. of my character from gossip in the past I have brought back to you, and not only that, if something is too hot for you to hold, seriously now tell me what did you think I was going to do?

Besides, the bible says "my people are destroyed for lack of knowledge" so I've made it my personal business to become the local gossip college.

Yes! I love me some gossiping I'm not ashamed to say, that's me. Gossiping doesn't cost me a dime, in fact, gossiping is free.

But would you believe one day I heard some gossip and guess what, it had the nerve to be all about me. It makes no different rather it was true or not, but I can tell you my spirit was no longer free.

I've learned that gossip is a powerful tool that is used by our untamed tongue. It has been proven to be a weapon just as dangerous as a loaded gun.

So the next time before you begin to spread some gossip, think about all the harm it can do. Then ask yourself one simple question, is that something you would want others to speak on or gossip about you?

How Do I Let Go

I know how I got caught up, but how do I let go?

When I have been so long in this predicament and it's the only thing I know.

I am desperately crying out and I am making a plead.
My mind is so tired and my spirit is very grieved.

I know I did this to myself that much I do know.
But please can someone tell me, how do I let go?

I Just Wanted To Say Thank You

Life sometimes has a way of taking a turn in ways you would have never expected. Sometimes you are left feeling lonely, alone and even a little neglected.

You try your best to keep a smile on your face and laugh when others think something is funny. You say to yourself I will make it through this day, even though I lack joy, peace and money.

I don't want to make this poem all about me neither the things that I've been through. This is a poem of gratitude, I just wanted to say thank you.

I thank you for thinking of me and my family in each dilemma we have found ourselves in. You could have been very judgmental and said, those were our trials and tribulations and they could have been due and caused by our own personal sin.

I'm sure there have been times when you have blessed my family with money, that money could have been spent to meet your personal need. My prayer for you is, that you would never be in want, and that God would bless you, your spouse, your children and their seed.

I want you to know, I don't take it lightly neither do I take it for granted that, that was something you had to do. I am so grateful you have been a blessing unto me, so I just wanted to say, thank you.

It is always good to know you are not alone in the struggles of life you go through. And the hurt and pains that you are feeling, someone is there to share them with you.

I don't think you fully understand how much of a blessing you were during the times of my endeavors and how your concern helped to see me through. In words of short, but very heartfelt, I just wanted to say, thank you.

When Death Has Called My Name

When death has called my name, please for me don't you cry. To be absent from this world is to be present with my Lord and Savior that sits on high.

Those tears that you shed let them be for you. Cry if you must, but please think things through.

When you think of me let it generate a smile. Don't think of my test, afflictions, tribulations or trials.

We are all here on this earth only for an appointed time. Whether our days are long or short, it is up to Jesus who is still divine.

So once again cry if you must, but my soul is resting in the Lord. I no longer have to fight, I have laid down my shield and sword.

For to be absent from this body, heaven I will gain. And that can only happen when death has called my name.

No Limit

There is no limit to what God can do. He has healed others He can heal you too.

By His strikes we are healed according to His word. So trust and believe in what He will perform to be nothing less than superb.

I love you and wish you well so all the world you can tell.

How God has healed and brought you through. Now there's nothing you cannot do.

Extraordinary Love

I am a firm believer that there is a God up above, because He has given you for me; such an extraordinary love.

You hung in there with me when I lost my way and when all I thought about was pleasing self night and day.

I took your love for granted and I tossed it to the side. My actions often spoke, speak not, if you want to be with me just come along for the ride.

I know there were more times than not when your heart was crushed and you tried to communicate through words or deeds. But I was too selfish, loving on myself, not being concern about your wants or your needs.

I know your days must have been long and your nights very lonely, because I took the love we once shared and kept it for me only.

I am deeply sorry for the challenges I have taken you through. I thank God for another chance and for days that are brand new.

Thank you for being dedicated and the phenomenal woman that you are, my daily prayer is, thank you Lord, I didn't leave a scar.

You are truly a blessing, and you deserve the best and for the rest of our lives I will give you nothing less.

I love you and I thank you for being a woman who is able to stand the test of time, because sometimes it only take one little mistake to leave your mate behind.

So once again I thank my heavenly father that sits high up above, for giving you, for me, such an extraordinary love.

Jealousy

Jealousy is an ugly demonic spirit. The bible says it is as cruel as the grave. It can make an average person or a renowned achiever become cold hearted, bitter, judgmental and full of rage.

Jealousy can be found in the streets, amongst your friends, in the churches, but most sadly in your home. Jealousy will eat you alive if you entertain it for too long.

Jealousy has its way of being deceptive by making you believe everything you say or do towards an individual is alright. But if the truth be told and if you are really honest with yourself you know some of the things you say or do toward that person are said or done out of spite.

You may not know the individual personally or they may be a friend or a family member that is connected to you. However, when jealousy has concealed and embedded itself in your heart it doesn't matter who it is, because doing anything right towards that person has now become hard to do.

It has been said that jealousy is a resentment against a person, success or advantages or it may be caused by just who that person is. But have you ever thought about the pain, the suffering or the struggles that that person had to endure, to become who they are or accomplish what they have, whether their struggle was one day or many years.

So, before you continue to allow jealousy to be the ruler of your life: think hard about what you would have to sacrifice, and that is the joy of the Lord which is the essence of your peace of mind. There is nothing on earth that could ever substitute that joy, because it is in a class all by itself, it is one of a kind.

My Prayer

Heavenly Father,

I thank you for choosing and counting me worthy in spite of my humanly flaws and imperfections as a person, as one of the vessels you have decided to use to help to be an encouragement in the lives of your people.

Because I trust in you Lord, I feel it is safe to say, I thank you for the many lives that have been changed for the better through these poems. I take no credit for you allowing me to help plant the seed, because I realize it is you who do the cultivating. So, Lord I give you all the glory and honor for every poem that has been written and formed into this book.

For I know this book has been designed by you to help lead someone into salvation: to edify, to encourage, to instruct as well as construct, for uplifting, for strengthening, and for the peace and joy of your people. So, Lord I thank you once more that through these poems something has been embedded in the spirit of the reader or hearer that will last in their hearts and minds a life time.

Amen.

Author's Contact Information

luriatye@att.net

luriainspirational.wordpress.com

www.ingramcontent.com/pod-product-compliance
Lightning Source LLC
Chambersburg PA
CBHW051659090426
42736CB00013B/2442